The Ways of God

St. Thomas Aquinas

The Ways of God

SOPHIA INSTITUTE PRESS
Manchester, New Hampshire

The Ways of God is an English translation of *De divinis moribus* by St. Thomas Aquinas. The translation was made by Raissa Maritain and Margaret Sumner and published as *The Divine Ways* by the Basilian Press in London, Ontario, in 1946. This 1995 edition includes minor corrections and revisions to the Maritain/Sumner translation.

Sophia Institute Press

Box 5284, Manchester, NH 03108

1-800-888-9344

Nihil Obstat: Rev. W. T. Flannery, S.T.D.
Imprimatur: John T. Kidd, D.D.
London, Ontario, March 7, 1942

Library of Congress Cataloging-in-Publication Data

Thomas, Aquinas, Saint, (1225?-1274).
    [De divinis moribus. English]
    The Ways of God / St. Thomas Aquinas.
       p. cm.
    Originally published: The divine ways. Windsor, Ont. Christian Culture Press, Assumption College, 1942.
    ISBN 0-918477-30-1 (pbk. : alk. paper)
    1. God—Attributes. I. Title.
BT130. T56 1995   95-36706
231'.4—dc20   CIP

95 96 97 98 99 10 9 8 7 6 5 4 3 2 1

Contents

Preface

This beautiful meditation is *Opusculum 62* of the Roman edition of the *Works of St. Thomas Aquinas* (published in Latin in 1570 by order of Pope Pius V). It was introduced to the English-speaking world in a 1942 translation by Margaret Sumner and Raissa Maritain, wife of the internationally known Thomistic scholar, Jacques Maritain.

Although *The Ways of God* was included in the 1570 edition of St. Thomas's works, modern scholars have been unable to document with academic certainty that it was actually written by St. Thomas himself.

Remarking on this, Raissa Maritain in her 1946 edition made the observation: "If it is not actually by the hands of St. Thomas, it is, in any case, the faithful interpreter of his doctrine, and its elevated spirit as well as its candor render it worthy of being placed under the name of the Angelic Doctor."

We agree; and for this reason we are pleased to make this little work available once again to the English-speaking public.

The Publisher

The Ways of God

NOTE: The biblical quotations in these pages follow the enumeration found in the Douay-Rheims edition of the Old and New Testaments. Quotations from the Psalms and some of the historical books of the Bible have been cross-referenced with the differing names and enumeration in the Revised Standard Version, using the following symbol: (RSV =).

The ways of God

"Be ye perfect as your heavenly Father is perfect."[1] Holy Scripture never orders and never counsels us to do the impossible. By these words, then, the Lord Jesus does not command us *to accomplish* the very works and ways of God, which no one can attain in perfection.

But He invites us *to model ourselves* on them, as much as is possible, by applying ourselves to imitate them. We can do this with the help of grace and we should do so. And as the Bishop John said, nothing is more suitable to man than to imitate his Creator, and to carry out, to the degree that he is able, the will of God.

[1] Matt. 5:48.

The immutability of God

In God, there is a primary perfection, which is that He never changes in His nature.

God Himself declares this by the prophet, "I am God and I do not change,"[2] and by Saint James: "Every best gift, and every perfect gift, is from above, coming down from the Father of lights, with whom there is no change, nor shadow of alteration."[3]

Created things bear in themselves a trace of this changelessness, in that they are not changeable in their essence; consider, for example, angels, the soul, the heavens, and the four elements.

[2] Cf. Mal. 3:6.
[3] James 1:17.

And if sometimes God sends His angels, and sometimes does not send them; if at times He withdraws His grace and at times confers it; if now He punishes sins, and now cloaks them, the change is in creatures, but not in the Creator.

In short, the changelessness of God's decrees with regard to the good and the bad will confirm itself at the last day, when He will give forever to the good a recompense superior to their merits, and will inflict forever on the bad a punishment that is less than the gravity of their sins.

Our own constancy

Let us strive therefore to acquire stability of spirit, in order that, broken by adversity or tempted by prosperity, we never depart from the right way, that we may say with Job, "My justification, which I have begun to hold, I will not forsake; for my heart doth not reproach me in all my life,"[4] and with Saint Paul, "For I am

---

[4] Job 27:6.

sure that neither death, nor life, nor angels, nor
principalities, nor powers, nor things present,
nor things to come . . . shall be able to separate
us from the love of God."[5]

But, alas, how inconstant we are in holy
meditations, in lawful affections, in steadfast-
ness of conscience, and in a right will. Ah, how
suddenly we pass from good to bad, from hope
to groundless fear, and from fear to hope, from
joy to unreasonable grief, and from sadness to
vain joy, from silence to loquaciousness, from
gravity to trifling, from charity to rancor or to
envy, from fervor to tepidity, from humility to
vainglory or to pride, from gentleness to anger,
and from joy and spiritual love to carnal love
and pleasure.

In this way we never remain one single
instant in the same condition, unless, alas, we
are constant in inconstancy, in infidelity, in
ingratitude, in spiritual defects, in imperfection,

[5] Rom. 8:38-39.

in negligence, in frivolity, and in ill-regulated thoughts and affections. Even the motions that trouble our exterior senses and our limbs reveal our interior instability.

Nevertheless, we should work without ceasing to acquire constancy of soul, so that we may conduct ourselves in all circumstances with the qualities of equanimity, maturity, and sweetness.

The delight of God in goodness

In God, there is another perfection: all goodness is pleasing to Him by nature, always and everywhere, whether it be in angels, in men, or in other creatures.

This goodness includes qualities of the body (like beauty, strength, grace, sweetness, and the fullness of natural maturity), qualities of the soul (such as perspicacity of the spirit, tenacity of memory, subtlety of the intelligence, rectitude of the will, and freedom of the will), and natural gifts (such as the ability to read well, to sing well, to preach well, to be eloquent, sober, and continent, and to have well-regulated habits). Finally, these goods include the gifts of grace, which please God above everything – gifts such as faith, hope, charity, humility, patience, mercy, obedience, truth, temperance, justice, prudence, and knowledge.

Similarly all evil displeases God everywhere and always and in whatever it exists. As justice is the enemy of injustice and impurity of purity, so the malice of man opposes the goodness of God, because it lessens or even completely destroys the divine good that grace gives to nature.

Our own delight in goodness

All that is good should also please us, always and everywhere and in every creature. We must protect and support goodness with solicitude, and resist boldly those who combat it.

We should always and everywhere detest evil with all our heart and exert ourselves to prevent it because it is injurious to God and harmful to one's neighbor; and much more because of the insult to the Creator than because of the danger to man.

But, alas, more often it is the opposite that takes place. For if we feel sad because someone is praised and loved on account of his humility, his piety, his devotions, or his other gifts, and if we try to diminish his merits, what do we show ourselves to be if not beings whom goodness does not please?

And when we converse with slanderers and laugh with them, when we delight in these frivolities and other faults of the same order, what do we do, if not confirm that evil things do not displease us?

The foreknowledge of God

In God, there is another perfection. He foresees with prudence all future things, good or bad. Before they happen, He knows them and sees the good or the evil that will result from them.

God foresaw the fall of the angel Lucifer and that of the first man. He permitted temptation; He knew in advance all the evil that would result from it for the human race, and also all the good – that is to say, the Incarnation of the Son of God, by which man receives a glory even greater than that which he had before the Fall.

Our own foresight

Let us also foresee all our doings, our words, our desires, our works, and let us consider the good and the evil that may result for us from them, as well as the scandal or edification that others will receive from them. Likewise, let us ponder beforehand the temptations that will perhaps arise from demons or from men, from our friends according to the flesh or according to the spirit, and how we should resist them, endure them, or flee them. For expected darts wound us less severely.

We must also foresee what will happen at the moment of the separation of our soul from our body, the sufferings of our body, the anguish of our soul, and the greatness of the peril, and likewise where we shall dwell, with God or with the Devil, in Heaven or in Hell.

It is useful for us to keep in mind the great joy of those who dwell with God and the tremendous misery of those who have departed from Him. So Moses desired: "Oh, that they would be wise and would understand, and would provide for their last end."[6]

---

[6] Deut. 32:29.

The forbearance of God

In God, there is another perfection, which is that no matter how grave the outrages and disdain that He receives from His creatures, He never hates human nature itself. On the contrary He loves it truly and desires its well-being ardently, although He detests the evil that is within it.

God provides for all the temporal needs of His creatures without even waiting until they ask Him for them, and He grants spiritual gifts to those who desire them. "For He makes the sun to shine on the good and on the bad; and He makes the rain to fall on the just and on the unjust."[7]

[7] Matt. 5:45.

Our own forbearance

We also should strive toward this perfection, in order that no matter how grievously a man has injured us, we never hate his nature, but that, wishing him every kind of good, we should be always ready to grant to him at once whatever corporal and spiritual help he expects from us.

But there is in God a just hatred that we also should partake of; for it is necessary that the love we have for man should not extend to loving his sin, no more than we should detest human nature because we detest its vices. On the contrary, let us love the nature and hate its vices.

The justice of God

In God, there is another perfection, which is
that the malice of one person never damages, in
the judgment of God, the good that is in another. Thus the fall of Lucifer did not harm the
Archangel Michael, and the perfidy of Judas did
not lessen the charity of the blessed Peter.

Our own justice

But we, miserable as we are, if a monk is
guilty of some excess, we reproach with the
fault of one individual the whole monastery and
the entire Order and even every monk without
exception.

If one of our enemies offends us, we pursue
a great number of innocent people with our
hatred, including all his descendants, friends,

and associates. That is something that the law of God forbids. "The soul that sinneth, the same shall die; the son shall not bear the iniquity of the father, and the father shall not bear the iniquity of the son; the justice of the just shall be upon him, and the wickedness of the wicked shall be upon him."[8] "For everyone shall bear his own burden."[9]

And how often does it not happen, when our soul is troubled, that we blame God Himself, who certainly does not deserve it? For then we no longer wish to sing nor study, nor read, nor pray.

[8] Ezek. 18:20.
[9] Gal. 6:5.

The rectitude of God

In God, there is another perfection, which is that He never omits nor puts aside mercy for justice, or justice for mercy. In fact, God never judges or condemns without mercy and when He pardons, justice is never wounded.

Our own rectitude

But if we try to practice justice, mercy dies in our soul; and if we show mercy, justice is buried. But Scripture recommends both justice and mercy: "May mercy and truth never abandon thee."[10] And the Psalmist said, "I will sing of mercy and of justice before Thee, O Lord."[11]

[10] Prov. 3:3.
[11] Ps. 100:1 (RSV = Ps. 101:1).

The longanimity of God

In God, there is another perfection. At times, all the saints and all creatures cry vengeance against the sinner, as is written in the book of Revelation: "How long, O Lord (holy and true) dost Thou not judge and revenge our blood on them that dwell on the earth?"[12]

God, however, with patience and mercy awaits the sinner until his death in order to have pity upon him, should he, even in this last moment, regret his evil ways and turn toward Him. For the Lord who is merciful does not rejoice in the loss of the living.

[12] Rev. 6:10.

Our own longanimity

But we, in our impatience, before the grave is even dug for the sinner, cursing him and crying out for justice, would like to see him swallowed up at that very instant. We reproach God for bearing so long with the evil that the wicked cause the just to suffer, and we do not wish to consider the good that His wisdom expects to draw even from the malice of the impious.

For in His forbearance with the wicked, the Lord is as good and as worthy of praise as if He had preserved the world from sin or delivered it completely from evil.

This forbearance is a testimony to God's omnipotence. For it requires no great power to cast the wicked into the depth of Hell, but it demonstrates God's tremendous mercy to take pity on and spare the sinner.

The bounty of God

In God, there is another perfection: for He communicates to creatures all the good that in its essence is communicable and that they have the capacity to receive, and does this continuously, as soon as they allow Him to give it, even though He sees that His gifts do not come to fruition in them.

God united human nature and the divine nature in the person of the Word, the greatest work of all. And aside from His many other spiritual gifts, God has made the human soul capable of receiving the Trinity within itself, and He nourishes it with the flesh and blood of His beloved Son. God withheld nothing that could be given, and this is the property of divine goodness. That which He possesses by His nature,

The Ways of God

God communicates to creatures by grace: bliss
to the angels, without their having known misery; power to the Apostles, in such a way that
all that they shall bind or unbind on earth shall
be bound or unbound in Heaven; the fore-
knowledge of all things to come to prophets;
fortitude in the face of adversity to martyrs; constancy in prosperity and failure to confessors;
and continence amid the seductions of the flesh
to virgins.

God also shares spiritually with some indi-
viduals the blessings that He has by His nature.
He gave magnanimity to Abraham; meekness
to Moses, the gentlest of men; the stewardship
of Egypt to Joseph; strength to Samson; zeal for
justice to Eli; patience to Job and to Tobias;
power to raise the dead to Elisha; wisdom in
judgments to Daniel; faithfulness to Samuel;
mercy toward his persecutors to David; prudence to Solomon; love of holiness and truth
to John the Baptist; humility to the Blessed
Virgin; charity to Peter; chastity to John; zeal

for souls and the understanding of things above
to blessed Paul. Each one distinguished himself
in the exercise of his special gift, while possess-
ing also the other virtues.

Our own bounty

And we, not only should we give to one
another our eyes, that they may see for others;
our ears that they may hear confessions; our
mouths, that they may be ready to preach and
to counsel; our feet, that they may walk in serv-
ice of our neighbor; and our hearts that they
may meditate upon the salvation of others. But
also we should give all that we possess of spiritual or temporal goods.

All that we can do outwardly by our works
and inwardly by our desires, all that we are in
body and in soul, we should give generously to
each of those who are in Purgatory and to those
who are now alive and who soon will be gone,
in order that they may live according to the will
of God now and forever.

The forgiveness of God

In God, there is another perfection, which inclines Him to forgive immediately the gravest and most numerous offenses, if we make a firm resolution to turn from them and truly to amend.

Even more, God forgets these offenses in return for a single lamentation of a contrite heart, as Scripture says.[13] And if we remain in this good will, He does not contemplate vengeance for our sins later, nor does He contemplate reproaching us with them in order to dismay us, nor charging us with them in order to love us less, nor driving us away from Him by withdrawing His intimacy.

[13] Cf. Ps. 50:18-19 (RSV = Ps. 51:16-17).

Our own forgiveness

But we, who should walk in the footprints of God – it is with difficulty that we agree from the heart to forgive a single small offense of one who implores our forgiveness!

If it happens that we do forgive, we almost never forget; we rejoice in the embarrassment of our debtor; we have small pity for him in adversity; or else we love him less than we did before. If we do not reproach him it is certain, however, that we exclude him from our intimacy, and that even in times of trial we refuse him our counsel and our support.

We should, on the contrary, forget the offenses of our enemy, even though he neither repents nor amends, in imitation of Christ who prayed for those who crucified Him, and who, far from repenting, mocked Him.[14] Nothing makes us more like God, said Saint John

[14] Luke 23:34.

Chrysostom, than to allow ourselves to be easily
appeased and to be pitiful to the wayward and
to those who harm us. For the height of perfection is to love our enemies, and to pray for
them as did the Lord Jesus.

The mercy of God

In God, there is another perfection. He exacts nothing that is beyond our strength in fasting, prayers, vigils, almsgiving, bodily mortifications, regular discipline, and similar things.

And if we fail in great and difficult works to efface our sins, God is contented with the most humble things, such as tears that come from the heart. It is thus He considered the tears of Hezekiah, and revoking the sentence of death that He had pronounced upon him by the prophet Isaiah, He granted him fifteen more years of life.[15]

He listened, with the same mercy, to the tears of blessed Peter, when at the cock-crow,

[15] 4 Kings 20:1-6 (RSV = 2 Kings 20:1-6).

he wept bitterly over the enormous fault of his denial.[16]

If it should happen that someone cannot weep, a single word, coming from a contrite heart, suffices for God. It is thus that to the robber who said to Him, "Lord, remember me when Thou shalt come into Thy Kingdom," Jesus replied, "This day thou shalt be with me in Paradise."[17]

And if someone lost the use of his tongue, God would accept fully the lamentations of his heart, as it is written in Scripture: "At whatever hour the sinner laments I will forget all of his iniquities."[18]

Finally, if illness deprived a man of the use of all his members, and even of the power to groan, before this extreme weakness God would even be contented with a will that is

---

[16] Luke 22:58-62.
[17] Luke 23:42-43.
[18] Cf. Jer. 31:34, 33:8.

good and sincere, in order to forgive the most grievous offenses.

Our own mercifulness

If a person has faithfully done as much as he is capable of doing, let us not exact more from him, whether he is secular or religious, even though by reason of his vocation he is bound to greater perfection.

The compassion of God

In God, there is another perfection: He reproaches no one for their natural defects of body (such as blindness, deafness, or deformity of the members) or for their defects of soul (such as stupidity, slowness, forgetfulness, irrationality, or natural timidity). For defects of this kind God does not disdain and does not reject any man.

But God does gravely charge us with those spiritual defects that are easy for each one to rise above with the help of grace, such as to take pride in the greatness of certain gifts, to desire superfluous things, to be sad at the progress of the just, to rejoice at their afflictions, to detest good works or to obstruct them, to vilify one's neighbor, to lessen his good reputation, to hold obstinately to one's preferences, to never renounce one's own opinion, to apply oneself to please man, to hate reprimand, to love adulation, to seek extraneous consolations, to cherish carnal affections, and the like.

Our own compassion

In the same way, we should never be contemptuous of those who are deprived of health, strength, beauty, eloquence, or charm in conversation — gifts that no one possesses of himself. Let us give thanks to God for those who possess these gifts. Let us be patient with the others, and let us try, as much as we are able, to supply all they lack.

The generosity of God

In God, there is another perfection, which leads
Him to grant His grace with extreme liberality
according to the calling of each one – as is said
in the Gospel: "And He gave to one five talents,
and to another two, and to a third a single one,
to each according to his capacity."[19]

Also, the more the heart of man is expanded
by love of God and of his neighbor, and the
more his meditations, his fervent prayers, his
just aspirations, his humility, and his generosity
have opened his soul to grace – the more elevated and greater is the grace that God the all-
powerful will bestow upon him. And indeed,
in the measure that a man seeks to conserve this

[19] Matt. 25:15.

grace and to use it for the praise of God and the common welfare, in the same measure will he receive a more abundant infusion of grace in this world and of glory in Paradise.

Our own generosity

Let us then open our hearts and prepare them by frequent resolutions in order that God, who is "rich in mercy to all who invoke Him,"[20] may shower His grace upon us according to His munificence.

But let him who is charged with dispensing spiritual goods by preaching and by counsels, watch with the greatest care that he does not give holy things to the dogs, and does not throw pearls before swine.[21]

"Day to day uttereth speech, and night to night showeth knowledge,"[22] which means that

---

[20] Ps. 85:5 (RSV = Ps. 86:5).
[21] Cf. Matt. 7:6.
[22] Ps. 18:3 (RSV = Ps. 19:2).

the more perfect things must be given to those who are perfect and the less perfect to those who are imperfect, as is the duty of a faithful steward.

It is thus, indeed, that Saint Paul announced Jesus to the imperfect, even Jesus crucified, but the mystery of wisdom contained therein he disclosed only to the perfect.[23] But let the man charged with the care of souls provide temporal goods to every poor man in accordance with what the latter needs — that is, in accordance with what he strictly requires, and no more.

[23] 1 Cor. 2:1-10.

The discretion of God

In God, there is another perfection; "He exacts much from him to whom He has given much, and even more from him to whom He has given more."[24]

From him whom God has blessed with temporal goods, He requires more abundant almsgiving to the poor; and from him who has received as his share health and strength, He demands more fasting and vigils.

From him for whom He has remitted a greater number of sins, or graver sins, and from him whom He has preserved from them, He awaits a more generous love and more worthy fruits of penitence.

[24] Luke 12:48.

41

The Ways of God

From him to whom He grants superior virtues, more perfect natural gifts of the spirit, of the intelligence, of the memory, and of the will, and to whom He provides more numerous and more elevated spiritual gifts (such as devotion, peace of conscience, spiritual joy, a firm and universal confidence, wisdom in discourse, fidelity in seeking perfection, diligence in good works, purity of intention, zeal for souls, and fervor in prayer), God lawfully requires greater acts of thanksgiving.

And from him whom God in His benevolence admits more often, and in a more intimate manner, to the knowledge of His goodness, eternity, immensity, omnipotence, liberality, charity, wisdom, mercy, justice, truth, faithfulness, patience, humility, sweetness, and nobility, He expects praise that is more abundant, more frequent, and more fervent.

From him whom God illumines in the quest for and knowledge of a higher perfection, in order that he shall practice it effectively and make more and more progress in it, God claims more. It is necessary as a result, that such a one by his words, his example, his prayers, and his desires, bring, as much as he is able, to the knowledge and practice of perfection those whom he judges capable of it.

Our own discretion

Let us watch therefore, in order that on the day of reckoning we may be able to render to God with interest each of the gifts He confides to us lest He should order them to be taken away from us, and to throw us miserably into outer darkness, with the lazy servant who had enveloped and hidden in a cloth the talent given to him by the Lord.[25]

[25] Matt. 25:24-30; Luke 19:20-26.

The just judgment of God

In God, there is another perfection, which is that He does not judge human acts on their exterior appearance; but He discerns all, in His immense and ineffable wisdom, according to the intentions of the heart. And it is according to the intention that gave birth to them that He accords to our works grave punishment or excellent recompense.

Our own just judgment

Neither, then, let us judge anyone's deeds on the testimony of our senses alone, on that which we see or hear.

Whether men show us an affable or a severe face, whether they speak to us with sweetness or with rudeness, whether they give us gifts or not, in every circumstance and as much as we can, let us be attentive not only to what they do, but to the intention that prompts them, and let us conduct ourselves accordingly.

For it is more useful to us to bear rude words from a true friend who proposes our amendment, than to listen to the sweet and flattering discourses of those who do not truly love us and whose only aim is to please us. "Wounds made by those who love us," said Solomon, "are better than lying kisses from those who hate us."[26]

[26] Prov. 27:6.

The truthfulness of God

In God, there is another perfection: He is true in His promises. According to God's own testimony, it is easier for Heaven and earth to pass away than that a single one of His words should change or cease to be true.[27]

For the Lord Jesus never speaks in vain, as we do, but each one of the words He has pronounced in time was said, in His wisdom, from all eternity.

And as He accomplished in coming among us the hidden predictions of the prophets concerning His Incarnation, His Nativity, His Passion, His Resurrection, His Ascension, and the mission of the Holy Spirit, so He will in the

[27] Mark 13:31.

very same way bring to pass the general resurrection that He has promised, as well as the future judgment.

He will remain faithful to what He has promised to the poor, when at the last day He will place them upon twelve thrones to judge the twelve tribes of Israel;[28] and faithful to what He has promised to those who weep, when He Himself will console them, as a mother consoles her children.[29]

Our Lord will hold to what He promised to the humble, when He will exalt them in the same measure that they had been abased and disdained; and to what He promised to the proud, when He will humble them as much as they had glorified themselves.[30]

And He will keep the promise that He made to the oppressed, when, at the command of His

[28] Cf. Matt. 19:28.
[29] Cf. Isa. 66:13; Matt. 5:5.
[30] Matt. 23:12; Luke 14:11.

Father, He will trample under His feet the neck of the oppressor.

"For God is faithful in all His words, and what He has promised He is powerful to accomplish."[31]

Our own truthfulness

Let us also be true and, first of all, let us keep faithfully the baptismal promises that our god-parents made in our name, and which oblige us to persevere in the Catholic Faith, to renounce the Devil and all his works, and to keep the Ten Commandments.

Let us also keep, in the same way, the vows we may have made of our own will later on – vows of obedience, of continence, of abstinence, of religion, and of similar things.

Let us be true in our dealings with our neighbor, that our speech may be "yes, yes; no, no."[32]

---

[31] Cf. Rom. 4:21; 1 Thess. 5:24.
[32] Cf. Matt. 5:37.

That is to say, let our hearts be always in accord with our lips.

Let us be faithful in our promises, and if we owe anything, no matter what it is, to a living person or to a dead one, let us free ourselves of our debt without any delay. For God demands the truth, and punishes severely those who despise it.

Alas, alas, how odious to men is this most excellent truth by which salvation comes to all. He who hates the truth, hates Christ. He hates truth; he betrays it; and not only does he betray the truth who proffers lies for truth, said Saint John Chrysostom, but he who does not speak the truth freely also betrays it, for it must be freely spoken; also he who does not defend it boldly, betrays it, for it must be boldly defended.

The perfect equity of God

In God, there is another perfection: He is no respecter of persons.[33]

Under the ancient Law, in fact, it was not the illustrious and the mighty, but obscure men like Moses, Joshua, and Gideon that God established as judges of His people.

Later He chose men of humble origin to reign, like Saul, son of Cis, and David, the least among his brothers, who tended the sheep.

When the Lord founded His Church, it was not nobles and men of great learning, but simple fishermen whom He established as princes over the whole earth, confiding to them the government of the Church. As the Apostle said:

[33] Acts 10:34.

"But the foolish things of the world hath God chosen, in order that He may confound the wise."[34]

Today it is the same. In dispensing His favors God does not consider men's power, strength, riches, or physical beauty. "Rather that man is pleasing to God no matter from what nation, who fears Him and performs works of justice."[35]

It is not only men who are handsome, rich, and illustrious, whom the Lord calls to eternal life. It is also the poor, the blind, the lame, and the weak whom He urges to enter in, and it is above all people of humble condition who progress in the Church of God and abound in spiritual graces.

At the Last Judgment the Lord will take no account of the person of kings and princes. He will judge with perfect equity the great and the lowly, and He will glorify each not according to

[34] 1 Cor. 1:27.
[35] Acts 10:35.

his power, nobility, and beauty, but according to his humility and charity.

Our own equity

Let us, then, keep ourselves from the respecting of persons. One must, as Saint Gregory said, honor man because He is man and made in the image and likeness of God, and not for anything that surrounds him (like riches, precious clothing, power, a noble name, or a multitude of friends and relations), for in the Holy Scriptures, respecting of persons is considered a great imperfection.

May one never hear, then, a preacher in his sermons praise the life of the rich and great who have their consolation on this earth, nor blame without reason the life of the poor and afflicted who suffer here below.

God grant that a confessor never listen more willingly to a person who enjoys the advantages of fortune, social rank, youth, or beauty, or from whom he expects some personal profit, rather than to a man who is old, poor, infirm, and of low birth, who might have greater need. May God also grant that he should not give more time and effort to the one than to the other. Or, if a confessor does occupy himself more intently with the former, let it be only because they are more exposed to sin than others, and because they can drag a greater number into evildoing.

And neither may it please God that those who distribute alms be respecters of persons. Instead, let the alms be more abundant in that place where the misery is the greatest; and let those who are progressing in virtue be aided more amply.

Nevertheless, in all circumstances one must act according to the teaching of the Apostle: "Render to each man his due . . . to one to whom fear is due, fear; to one to whom honor is due, honor."[36] To one to whom we owe love,

[36]Rom. 13:7.

let us give love; to one to whom we owe friendliness, let us render friendliness, in accordance
with both the degree of holiness and the dignity
of each.

The care of God for creatures

In God, there is another perfection: He takes care of all creatures, of the smallest as much as of the greatest, of the animals, the birds, and even of the sparrows, of which our Lord says, "Two sparrows sell for only a penny; even so, not one is forgotten by God."[37]

God maintains all living things in being and supplies unceasingly all their necessities. He takes care of the four elements, the plants and the trees that nourish themselves by them, and of all the animals, great and small, who dwell upon the earth, in the air, or in the waters.

But above all God takes care of men, who are created in His image and likeness. He made

[37] Cf. Matt. 10:29.

them members of His beloved Son and temples of the Holy Spirit. He has sent to each one an angel to watch over him. He gives life to them in the precious flesh and blood of His only Son. And what is more remarkable, God provides the necessities of life more abundantly to sinners, who are His enemies, than to those who are His friends.

God takes care of the souls in Purgatory in permitting that they be rescued by the desires of the Church Triumphant, by the prayers of the Church Militant, and by the oblations of priests, even when they offer them unworthily and therefore would themselves deserve to be condemned.

And while prayers, almsgiving, fasting, and pilgrimages accomplished without charity are insufficient to efface the sins of those who practice these devotions, it is, nevertheless, permitted piously to believe that such works, offered for the souls in Purgatory, may obtain for them, by an effect of divine goodness, some relief and even the remission of their sufferings, on account of the merits that they possessed here below.

Finally, God takes great care of the holy angels, whom He has established in great bliss, and whom He has forever preserved from all experience of evil.

Our own care for creatures

Let us also care for creatures, using each one according to the order willed by God, lest at the day of judgment they testify against us.

Let us care for all men, taking to our hearts their joys and griefs, seeking to restrain them from wrongdoing and to comfort them in the Lord by our desires, our prayers, and our good example.

Let us also care for the souls in Purgatory, applying ourselves frequently to relieving their sufferings by works of mercy.

Let us care for the angels, so that they shall not, by our fault, lose the joy that they ought to receive from the progress we make in virtue, thanks to their good care and to their protection.

And last and above all, let us take tender care of God Himself, doing everywhere and always that which He most desires us to do and that for which He has particularly destined us.

The serenity of God

In God, there is another perfection: it is that nothing can disturb Him. And although Scripture often speaks of His anger and His fury, it only wishes by this to show Him taking vengeance on sin, or justly withdrawing His grace from His creatures.

But God Himself is entirely serene. He has no contrary. His simplicity is so perfect, He possesses in His own nature such felicity and such great joyfulness, that no disturbance can ever touch Him.

Our own serenity

We must, therefore, as much as possible, flee all that disturbs us, for grace cannot dwell in an agitated soul. But to keep inner peace we need ardent devotion to God and love "as strong as death,"[38] because these have in us an effect like death, so that, seeing the evil deeds of our neighbor, we do not see them; hearing words that could harm us or that are said against us, we do not hear them; and so our heart is not occupied with these things.

We must, in imitation of David, be like the blind, the deaf, and the dumb, and like men without feeling. "But I as a deaf man heard not, and as a dumb man not opening his mouth."[39]

Let us, then, give ourselves up faithfully and with fervor to the things of God, and leave each one to his own conscience, to the judgment of his superiors, and to the ultimate justice of God, who said, "Vengeance belongs to me and I will render it to men, according to their works, in the appointed time."[40]

---

[38] Song of Sol. 8:6.
[39] Ps. 37:14 (RSV = Ps. 38:14).
[40] Cf. Deut. 32:35.

Similarly, and as much as we can, let us avoid troubling others, lest they in turn trouble us, as often happens, and our conscience be tormented.

For God the omnipotent, who loves justice, will not leave unpunished at the last day actions that, by causing confusion, have diminished here below the number of holy meditations, right desires, prayers, and other good works, and that have in this way harmed Catholicity in Heaven, in Purgatory, or on earth.

The disinterestedness of God

In God, there is another perfection, which is that in all that He has done and arranged, He has entirely ignored all thought of His own interest. He has considered, uniquely, the abundance of His eternal and immense goodness, and ordered all for the greatest good of the angelic and the human creation.

In creating and preserving the heavens, the four elements, and all that they enclose, God does not consider His own interest, but rather what is advantageous for men and angels.

Whatever God ordains among His creatures (whether fair weather or storms, famine or abundance, health or epidemics) and whatever He does for men (whether He confers or withdraws His grace, whether He makes them healthy or sick, weak or strong, poor or rich; whether He makes them live or die, permits the good or the bad to reign, to succor or to afflict the poor, to judge with equity or to offend justice), He does all, He orders all, He permits all, because of His infinite goodness and in view of the common good of men.

Our own disinterestedness

In all our desires, prayers, fasting, almsgiving, in all our acts and words, and in all that we bear from God, let our intentions be pure. Without aiming at our interest, without seeking to please men, without fear of displeasing them, without even fixing our intention on what we might receive of grace in the present time and of glory in the time to come, we should only consider the admirable goodness of God and act purely and in the first place for it, and in the second place for the salvation of our neighbor.

The more our intention is pure and strongly directed toward God, the less we dwell upon our own advantages and even upon those of other men, and the more our works will be agreeable to God and profitable to all. But, alas, how much they will lose in value before God, and for all creatures, if we see in them any other thing than the pure goodness of the Lord.

"He will separate the grain from the straw with His fan," says the Gospel.[41] God's wisdom will separate the pure from the impure. He will gather up only the wheat in His barns, and He will burn the straw; that is to say, He will reward in Heaven and will allow to serve for the good of all only that which has, with a pure intention, been done, or omitted, or suffered for Him alone. "The Lord will reward me according to my justice," said David, "and will repay me according to the cleanness of my hands, as my hands shall have been pure before His eyes."[42]

[41] Matt. 3:12.
[42] Ps. 17:21 (RSV = Ps. 18:20).

The excellent works of God

In God, there is another perfection – namely,
that He has done all His works in an excellent
manner.

For the creation of Heaven and of earth, of
angels and of men, and of all other creatures, is
so perfect that it would be impossible to con-
ceive it better ordained.

Supremely perfect above all is the work of
the Redemption, which none other in Heaven
nor on earth would have been able to accomplish but God.

He carried wisdom to its summit when
He conquered the Devil through that wood by
means of which the Devil had triumphed – that
is, when He hid until the end the divine power
under the fragility of humanity. Because if the

demons had recognized Him, the Apostle says, "Never would they have crucified the Lord of glory"[43] – that is to say, they would not have persuaded the people to crucify Him.

And all that God does today – whether He chastises sins or cloaks them on account of repentance; whether He confers His graces on the elect or withdraws His graces from them; whether He acts toward the faithful soul, now familiarly or now as a stranger; whether the air be cold or warm; whether it rain or blow; whether the road be dry or humid; whether the fruits of the earth abound or perish – it is impossible that all this could be better at any given moment, because the immense wisdom of God by an extreme charity and benignity produces each thing at the very time it is needed.

God will also accomplish very perfectly the work of remuneration, when He will give to each sin and to each member that had been the

[43] 1 Cor. 2:8.

instrument of the iniquity, its just punishment according to the quantity and the gravity of the fault committed, and when He will recompense with justice each act of goodwill, each word, and each example, according to the intensity of the supernatural love that produced them.

Our own works

We also should take every care to conduct each of our activities as well as we can, doing them by the virtue of our Lord Jesus Christ, with all the desire of the Church Triumphant and Militant, and in the name of our Creator, as though our entire salvation and the praise of God and the welfare of all creation depended upon a single act that we do, as if we should never again do a like act, or never again do another act at all afterward.

For each time that an extraneous thought, a turning of the soul toward something else, introduces itself into our actions, the spirit relaxes in its present work.

The Ways of God

For example, when we are praying, if at this moment we suggest to ourselves that we must write, or undertake some other work, our attention to prayer lessens, and we soon leave what we had begun.

The benevolence of God

In God, there is another perfection, which leads Him to judge no man according to his past or future malice or goodness, but according to the present state of his soul. Therefore God did not condemn Paul on account of his previous malice, nor save Judas on account of his past justice.

Our own benevolence

But we miserable creatures, whatever be the progress that someone makes in virtue or in holiness, we do not omit to remind ourselves often of his past injustice. On the other hand, if the just man happens to turn aside from the way of justice in some one point, although it be one single time, even if he repents of it, we no longer remember his holiness.

The mercifulness of God

In God, there is another perfection, which is
that He never punishes twice for the same fault,
if a first chastisement suffices and if the fault be
corrected following the punishment.

Our own mercifulness

Yet we, miserable creatures that we are,
would inflict, if it were in our power, one hun-
dred quite terrible punishments for one single
injury that is done to us.

The ways of God
should be our model

The faithful soul should try with all its effort to model itself as much as is possible on the divine ways of which we have been speaking.

For the more a soul has been modeled on its Creator in this world, the more it will be like Him in the life to come; and the more it is like Him, the greater will be its bliss, the more it will give glory to God, and the more it will be useful to every creature.

From this moment on, it behooves the faithful soul to exult in joy, for it will possess these ways of God in life eternal, "when we shall be like unto Him and we shall see Him as He is."[44]

[44] 1 John 3:2.

A Prayer

O most gentle God, who, foreseeing our desire, have imprinted Your image in our soul, we pray You in the name of all that You are, and by all that You are, to deign also mercifully to imprint in us Your divine ways. We ask this in order that Your labor for us be not lost, and that our life be not in vain nor given over to peril, should we fail to employ for our true end the care that You have taken of us.

The ways of God
that we cannot imitate

In God, still other perfections are found, which, however, are not imitable and which we can only admire.

Thus God alone knows the secrets of hearts; He alone knows and loves Himself perfectly; He alone rejoices fully in Himself and finds in Himself the praise that is befitting; He alone is sufficient unto Himself and has need of nothing outside of Himself.

God alone is the one from whom all good proceeds, the one alone in whom the blessedness of all abides. God alone possesses immortality, and "inhabiteth light inaccessible";[45] He

[45] 1 Tim. 6:16.

alone was able to make something out of nothing; He alone maintains all things in being.

God alone remits sins. He alone knows the hour of judgment. He alone knows the number of the elect.

Blessed be God!

Amen.

Sophia Institute Press

Sophia Institute is a non-profit institution that seeks to restore man's knowledge of eternal truth, including man's knowledge of his own nature, his relation to other persons, and his relation to God.

Sophia Institute Press serves this end in numerous ways. It publishes translations of foreign works to make them accessible for the first time to English-speaking readers. It brings back into print books that have been long out of print. And it publishes important new books that fulfill the ideals of Sophia Institute. These books afford readers a rich source of the enduring wisdom of mankind.

Sophia Institute Press makes high-quality books available to the general public by using advanced technology and by soliciting donations to subsidize general publishing costs.

Your generosity can help us provide the public with editions of works containing the enduring wisdom of the ages. Please send your tax-deductible contribution to the address noted below. Your questions, comments, and suggestions are also welcome.

For your free catalog, call:
Toll-free: 1-800-888-9344

or write:

Sophia Institute Press
Box 5284
Manchester, NH 03108

Sophia Institute is a tax-exempt institution
as defined by the Internal Revenue Code,
Section 501(c)(3). Tax I.D. 22-2548708